Little People, BIG DREAMS®

ALBERT EINSTEIN

Written by
Maria Isabel Sánchez Vegara

Illustrated by
Jean Claude

Frances Lincoln
Children's Books

Once upon a time, there was a little Jewish boy born in Germany who took four years to say his first word. His name was Albert, and for some time, his little sister Maja was his only friend. No-one else had enough patience to wait for him to talk!

Albert was five when his father gave him a pocket compass, which instantly became his favourite toy. There was something magical in that magnetic needle: it always pointed North. He wanted to learn how it worked.

School was a bit of a nightmare for Albert. But back home, he loved diving into a pile of physics and maths books, trying to prove theories on his own. By the time he was a teenager, he had published his first scientific paper!

After studying maths and physics in Switzerland, Albert got a job at a patent office. In this place, amazing new inventions were recorded. But none were as groundbreaking as the idea he was working on at home.

Albert was a bit disorganised but, inside that brain, his thoughts were in perfect order. He came up with a formula that said that anything we can see and touch can be turned into energy. It became the most famous formula in the world.

His curiosity led him to explore space and time by mixing two original ideas, and he turned physics upside down with his Theory of Relativity. When he was proven right on an experiment, every university in the world wanted to meet this scruffy physicist.

Albert was awarded a Nobel Prize for discovering photons: the tiny particles that light is made of. Still, he didn't attend the ceremony. He was busy travelling from place to place, sharing his knowledge with other scientists and thinkers.

Every country in the world received Albert with honour. But, back home, a very different welcome awaited him. The Nazis had taken control of Germany. They planned to get rid of anyone who was not like them – especially Jewish people.

It was not just Albert who was in danger, but also many of his colleagues. Before moving to America with his family, he convinced governments and universities to hire Jewish scientists. Thanks to him, they could leave Germany, too.

When the war broke out in Europe, Albert feared
that the Nazis could use his discoveries to create the
most terrible weapon in the world: a nuclear bomb. He
sent a letter warning the President of the United States.

He always regretted signing that letter. It led to the United States making their own nuclear bomb! Albert had always stood for peace and thought science should only be used to do good. That's why he refused to be involved in the creation of such a weapon.

He became an American citizen and loved his new home. Still, he felt terrible about how the country treated his Black fellow citizens. Whenever he could, he wrote against racism and used his fame to speak out about it.

And by always questioning everything, little Albert became one of the most original minds of the 20th century – a genius who proved to the world that curiosity and imagination are more important than knowledge.

ALBERT EINSTEIN

(Born 1879 – Died 1955)

1888

c. 1905

Albert Einstein arrived to parents Hermann and Pauline on March 14th, 1879, in Ulm, Germany. Older brother to Maja, Albert grew up in a non-religious Jewish family. His father, Hermann, was a salesman and engineer and his mother Pauline ran the family household. As a young child, he had what was considered to be speech difficulties, and turned to classical music, learning to play the violin at a very early age. Albert felt alienated at his school, struggling with the school's rigid style. Soon, his family moved to Italy and Albert continued his education at Aarau, Switzerland. In 1896 he entered the Swiss Federal Polytechnic School in Zurich to be trained as a teacher in physics and mathematics. Unable to find a teaching post on graduating, he instead went to work at the Patent Office. In his spare

1933

1944

time, he read and he wrote, and in 1905 – Einstein's 'miracle year' – he penned a series of papers that changed our view of the universe forever. In The Theory of Relativity and beyond, Albert always appeared to have a clear view of the problems of physics and was determined to solve them. In 1921, he won a Nobel Prize in Physics, and his work laid the foundation for research into the evolution of the universe. As the Nazi Party rose to power in Germany, Albert migrated to America in 1933 and never returned to his home country. There, he used his platform to advocate for social justice, especially for Black Americans. Today, he continues to inspire generations of great thinkers across the world as one of the greatest physicists in the history of humankind.

Want to find out more about **Albert Einstein?**

Have a read of these great books:

Who was Albert Einstein? by Jess Brallier

The Story of Albert Einstein by Suzan B Katz

Brimming with creative inspiration, how-to projects, and useful information to enrich your everyday life, Quarto Knows is a favourite destination for those pursuing their interests and passions. Visit our site and dig deeper with our books into your area of interest: Quarto Creates, Quarto Cooks, Quarto Homes, Quarto Lives, Quarto Drives, Quarto Explores, Quarto Gifts, or Quarto Kids.

Text © 2021 Maria Isabel Sánchez Vegara. Illustrations © 2021 Jean Claude.

Original concept of the series by Maria Isabel Sánchez Vegara, published by Alba Editorial, s.l.u

Little People Big Dreams and Pequeña&Grande are registered trademarks of Alba Editorial, s.l.u. for books, printed publications, e-books and audiobooks. Produced under licence from Alba Editorial, s.l.u.

First Published in the UK in 2021 by Frances Lincoln Children's Books, an imprint of The Quarto Group.

The Old Brewery, 6 Blundell Street, London N7 9BH, United Kingdom.

T 020 7700 6700 **www.QuartoKnows.com**

A catalogue record for this book is available from the British Library.

ISBN 978-0-7112-5756-6

Set in Futura BT.

Published by Katie Cotton • Designed by Sasha Moxon

Edited by Katy Flint and Rachel Williams • Production by Nikki Ingram

Editorial Assistance from Alex Hithersay

Manufactured in Guangdong, China CC072021

1 3 5 7 9 8 6 4 2

Collect the Little People, **BIG DREAMS**® series:

FRIDA KAHLO	**COCO CHANEL**	**MAYA ANGELOU**	**AMELIA EARHART**	**AGATHA CHRISTIE**	**MARIE CURIE**	**ROSA PARKS**

AUDREY HEPBURN	**EMMELINE PANKHURST**	**ELLA FITZGERALD**	**ADA LOVELACE**	**JANE AUSTEN**	**GEORGIA O'KEEFFE**	**HARRIET TUBMAN**

ANNE FRANK	**MOTHER TERESA**	**JOSEPHINE BAKER**	**L. M. MONTGOMERY**	**JANE GOODALL**	**SIMONE DE BEAUVOIR**	**MUHAMMAD ALI**

STEPHEN HAWKING	**MARIA MONTESSORI**	**VIVIENNE WESTWOOD**	**MAHATMA GANDHI**	**DAVID BOWIE**	**WILMA RUDOLPH**	**DOLLY PARTON**

BRUCE LEE	**RUDOLF NUREYEV**	**ZAHA HADID**	**MARY SHELLEY**	**MARTIN LUTHER KING JR.**	**DAVID ATTENBOROUGH**	**ASTRID LINDGREN**

EVONNE GOOLAGONG	**BOB DYLAN**	**ALAN TURING**	**BILLIE JEAN KING**	**GRETA THUNBERG**	**JESSE OWENS**	**JEAN-MICHEL BASQUIAT**

GRETA THUNBERG

SKOLSTREJK
FOR
KLIMATET

ARETHA FRANKLIN

CORAZON AQUINO

PELÉ

ERNEST SHACKLETON

STEVE JOBS

AYRTON SENNA

LOUISE BOURGEOIS

ELTON JOHN

JOHN LENNON

PRINCE

CHARLES DARWIN

CAPTAIN TOM MOORE

HANS CHRISTIAN ANDERSEN

STEVIE WONDER

MEGAN RAPINOE

MARY ANNING

MALALA YOUSAFZAI

ANDY WARHOL

RUPAUL

MICHELLE OBAMA

MINDY KALING

IRIS APFEL

ROSALIND FRANKLIN

RUTH BADER GINSBURG

MARILYN MONROE

KAMALA HARRIS

ALBERT EINSTEIN

CHARLES DICKENS

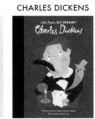

YOKO ONO

ACTIVITY BOOKS

STICKER ACTIVITY BOOK

COLOURING BOOK

LITTLE ME, BIG DREAMS JOURNAL

Discover more about the series at www.littlepeoplebigdreams.com

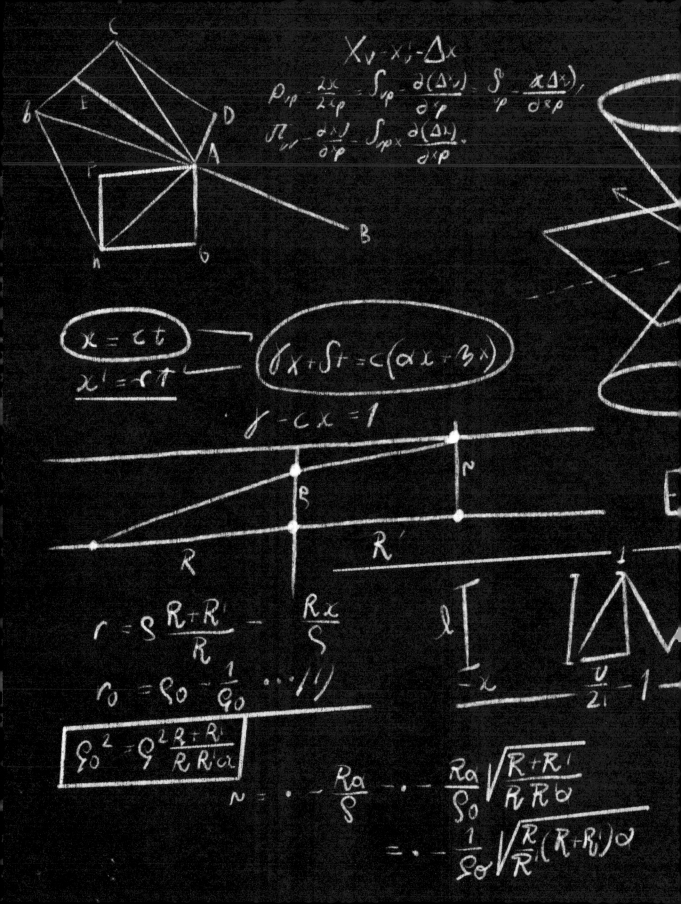

$$X_\nu - x_\iota - \Delta x$$

$$\rho_{\nu\varphi} - \frac{2x}{2^\varsigma\rho} = S_{\nu\varphi} - \frac{\partial(\Delta x)}{\partial^\varsigma\rho} - \frac{S}{\varphi} - \frac{x\Delta x)}{\partial^\varsigma\rho},$$

$$\Pi_{\nu\nu} - \frac{\partial x)}{\partial^\varsigma\rho} - S_{\eta\rho x} \frac{\partial(\Delta \iota)}{\partial^\varsigma\rho}.$$

$$x = ct$$
$$x' = ct'$$

$$\gamma x + St = c(\alpha x + \beta x)$$

$$\gamma - cx = 1$$

$$r = S\frac{R+R'}{R} - \frac{Rx}{S}$$

$$r_0 = \varrho_0 - \frac{1}{\varphi_0} \cdots //)$$

$$\boxed{\varsigma_0{}^2 = \varrho^2 \frac{R+R'}{R\,R'\alpha}}$$

$$n = \cdot - \frac{Ra}{S} - \cdot - \frac{Ra}{S_0}\sqrt{\frac{R+R'}{R\,R'b}}$$

$$= \cdot - \frac{1}{S_0}\sqrt{\frac{R}{R'}(R+R')\alpha}$$

$$\ell I$$

$$\frac{U}{2i} - 1$$